FIRST IMPRESSIONS
by ELVINA PEARCE
16 Original Piano Solos for Early-Level Pianists

These pieces offer refreshing and exciting repertoire that motivates students to excel. Here is innovative repertoire in five-finger positions that moves around the keyboard and utilizes pedal to help create big sounds. The descriptive titles are designed to capture the imagination and nurture interpretive skills. The pieces sound harder than they are and will give students a profound sense of accomplishment.

CONTENTS

Editor: Gail Lew
Production Coordinator: Karl Bork
Cover Design: Janel Harrison

Mystic Flute

ELVINA PEARCE

In the distance

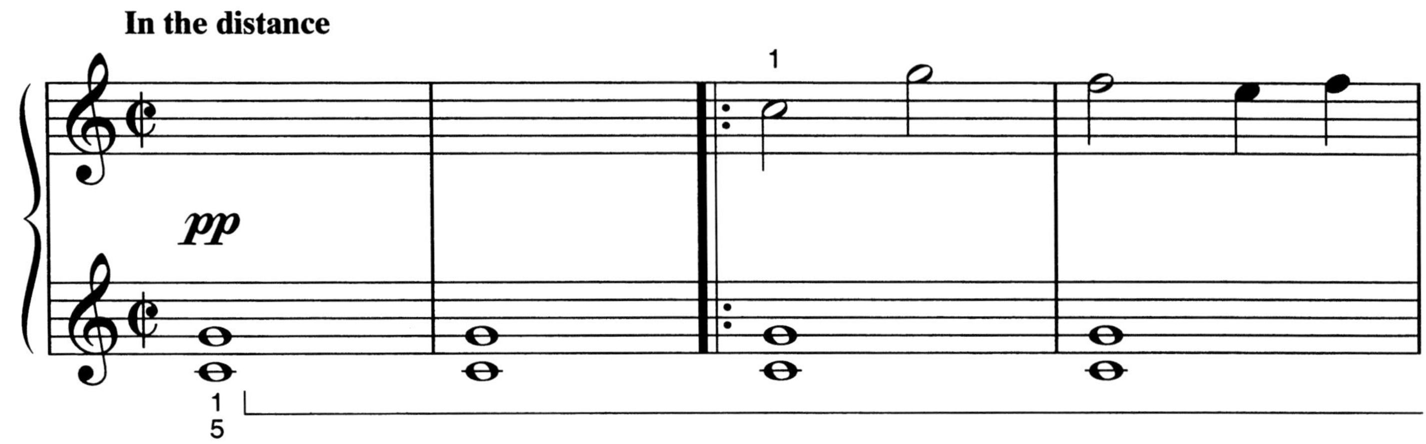

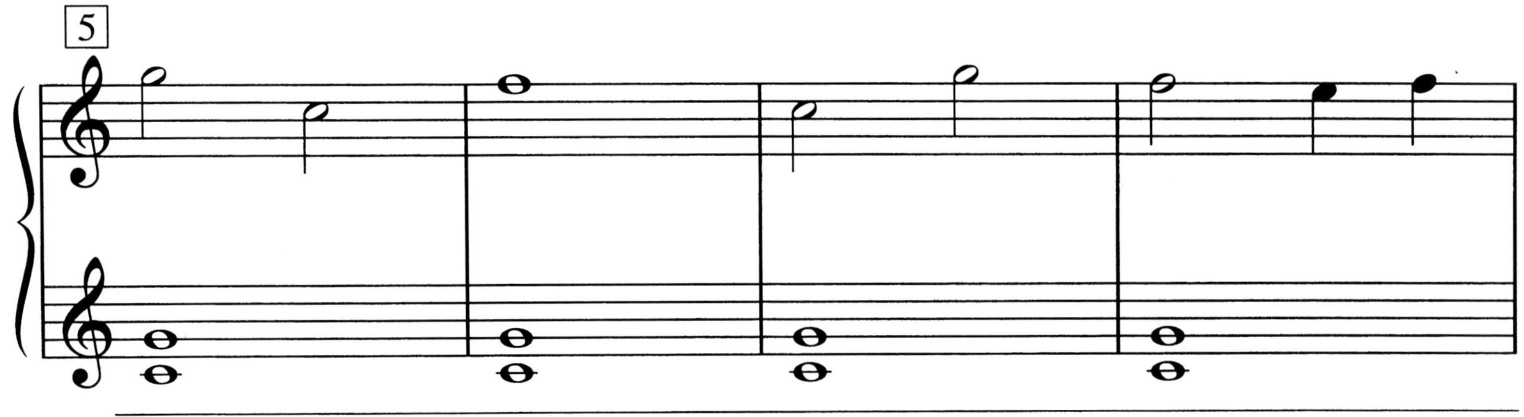

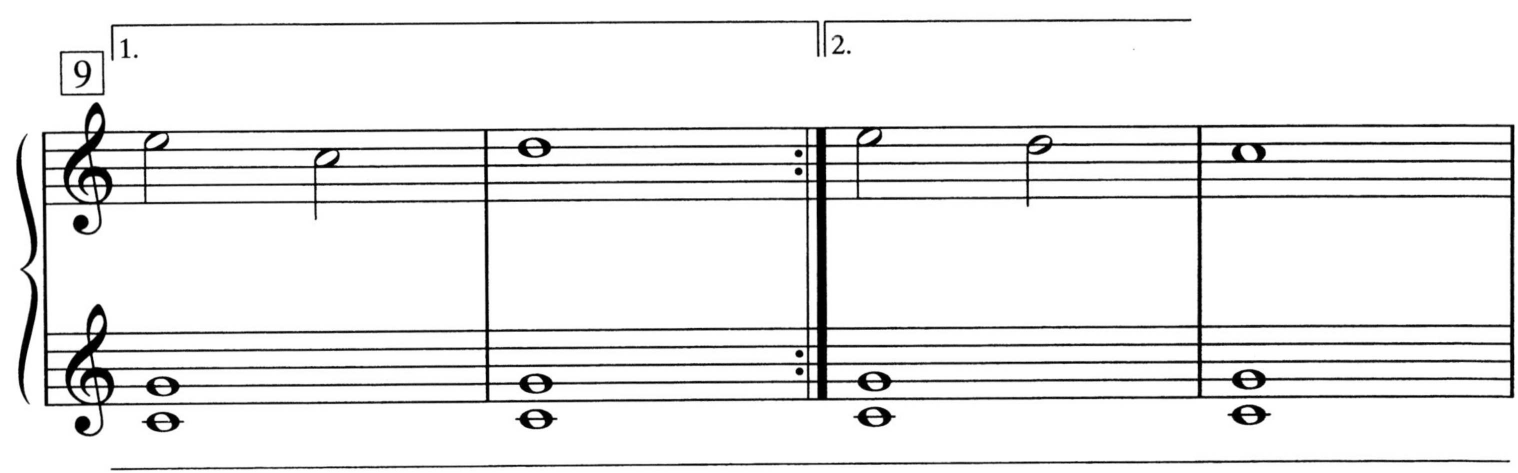

13
8va

16

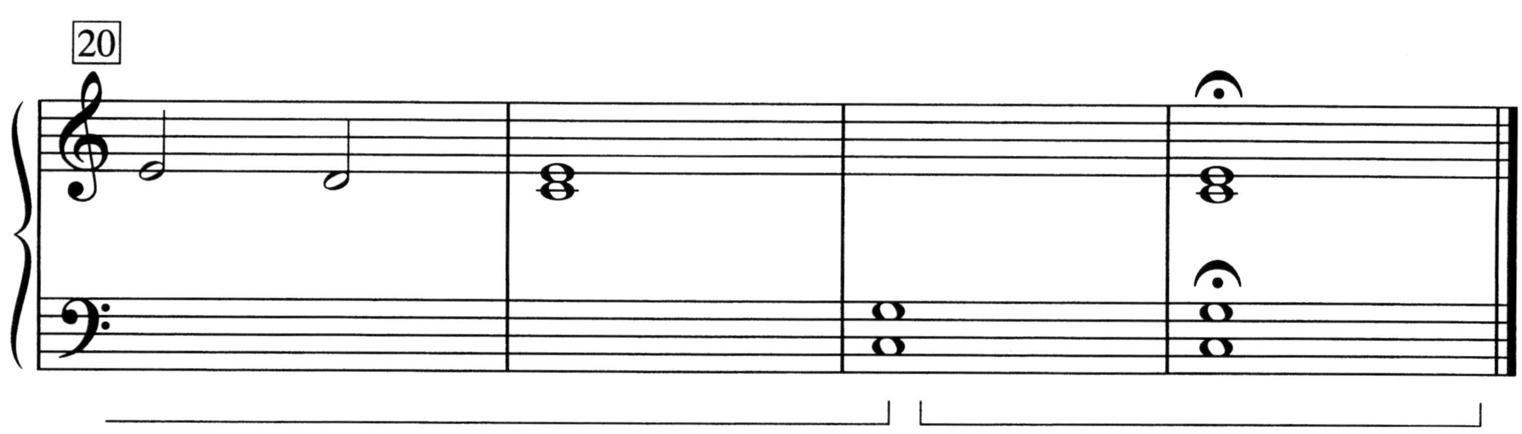

20

Heavy Load

Piggy-back

ELVINA PEARCE

Summer Evening

ELVINA PEARCE

The Hammock

ELVINA PEARCE

Scotch Plaid

Indian Portrait

ELVINA PEARCE

13
2
4

16
3
1
2
1
f

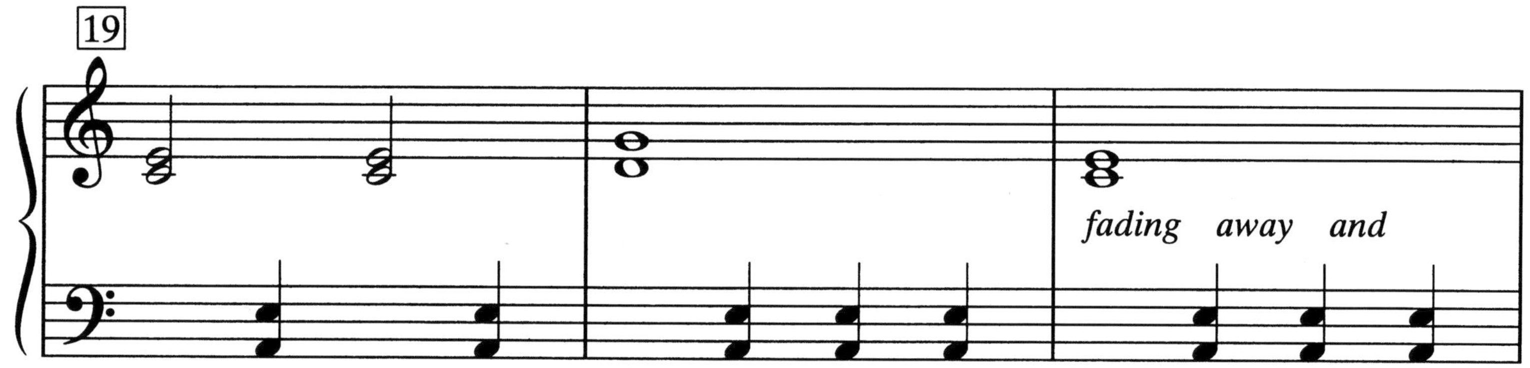
19
fading   away   and

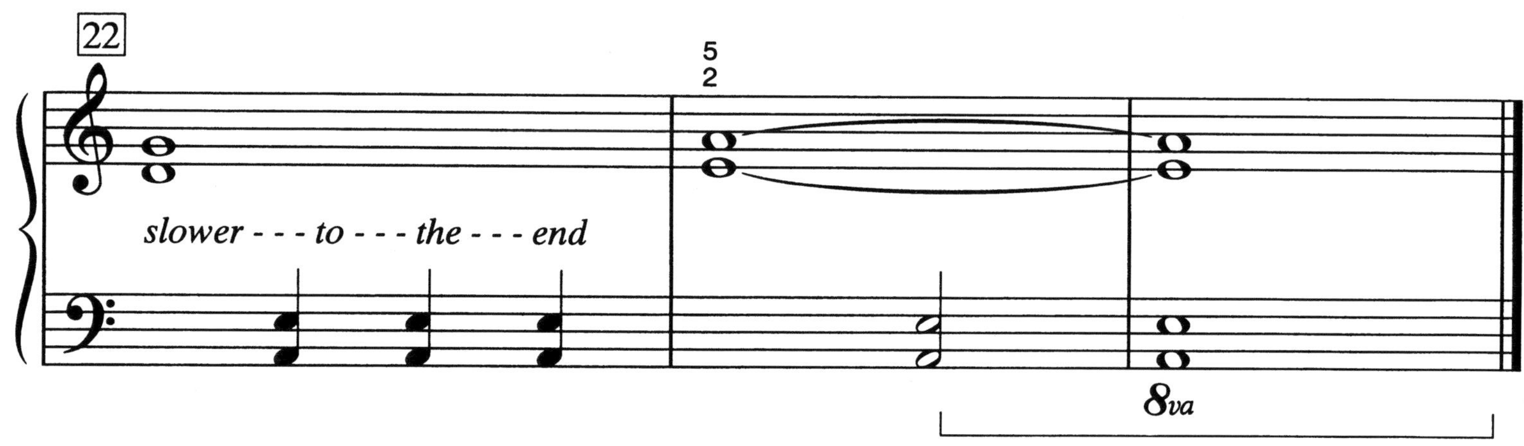
22
5
2
slower - - - to - - - the - - - end
8va

The Giant

ELVINA PEARCE

Ceremonial Dance

Moon March

ELVINA PEARCE

13
2
4
2
17
4
2
f
1.
21
2.
25
EL03218A

Drifting Sands

Jazzin' Blues

ELVINA PEARCE

Bouncin'

ELVINA PEARCE

2.
13
2
2
5
2
f
16
4
1
19
2
3
22
8va
2
5
2
p
f
8va
3
3
EL03218A

Black Swans

ELVINA PEARCE

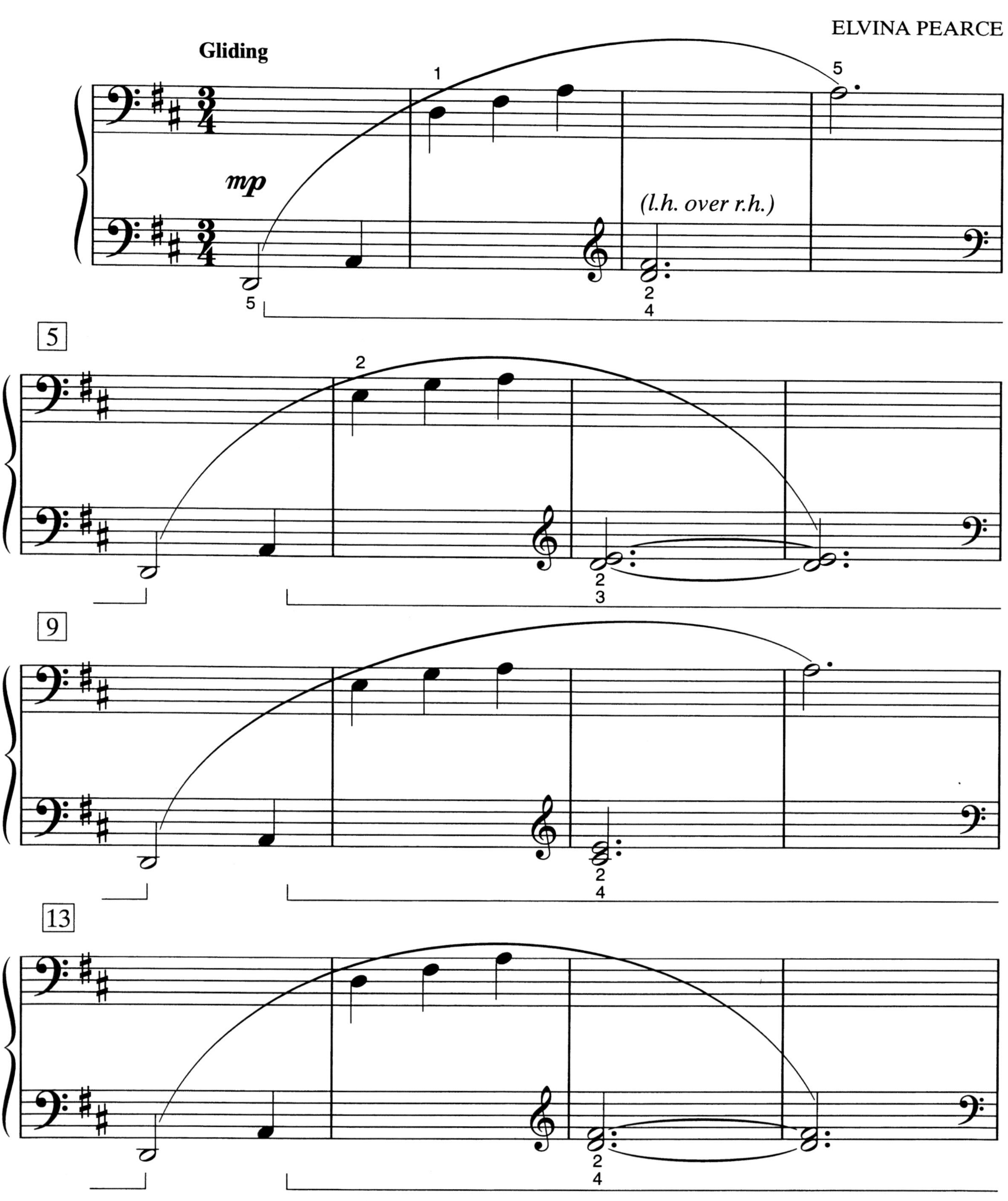

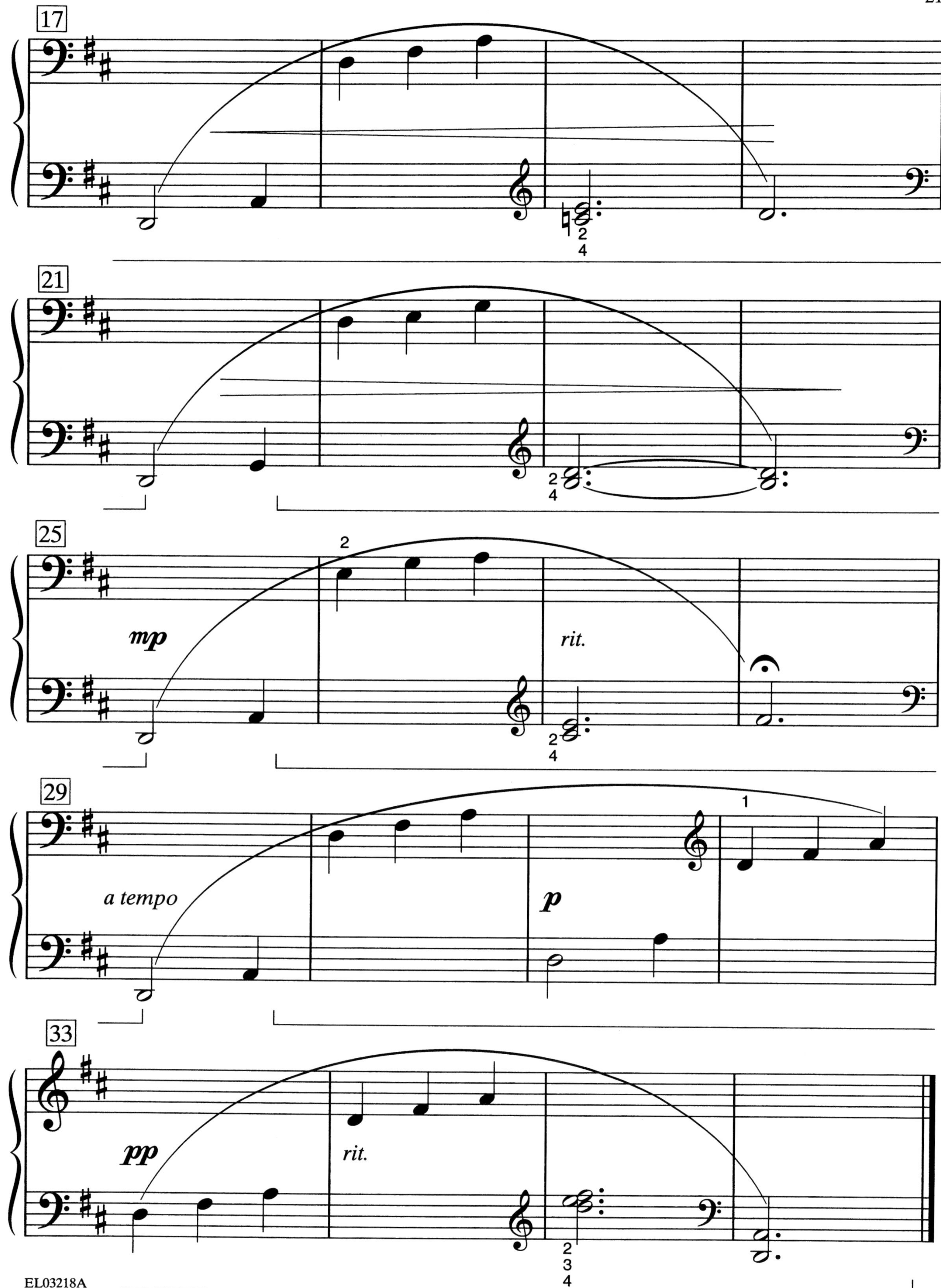
17
21
25
mp
rit.
29
a tempo
p
1
2
33
pp
rit.
EL03218A

Free Falling

ELVINA PEARCE

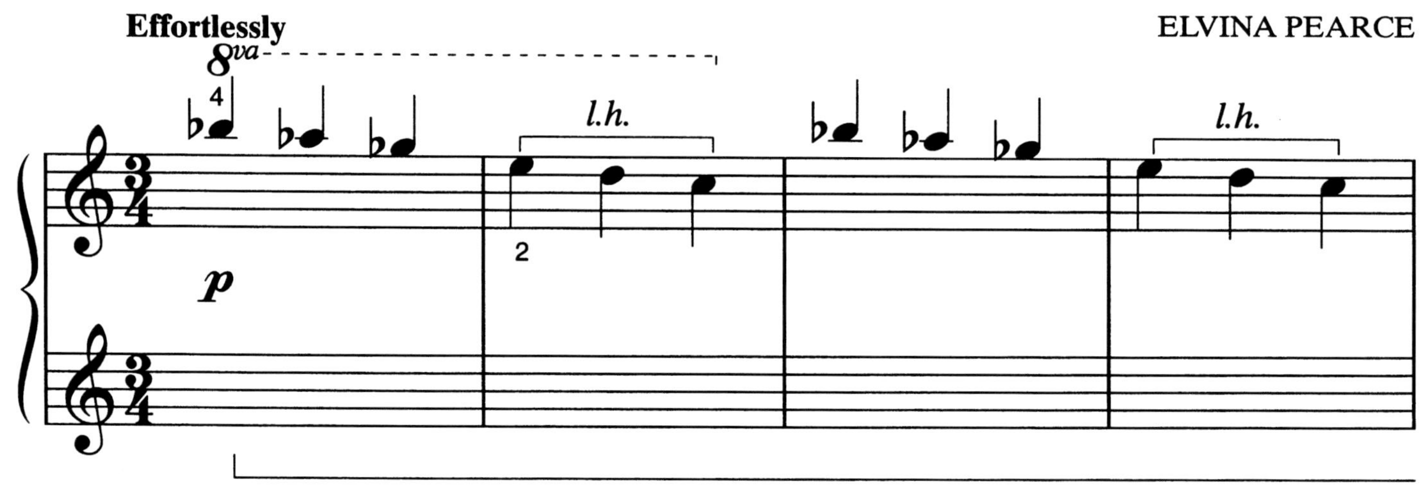

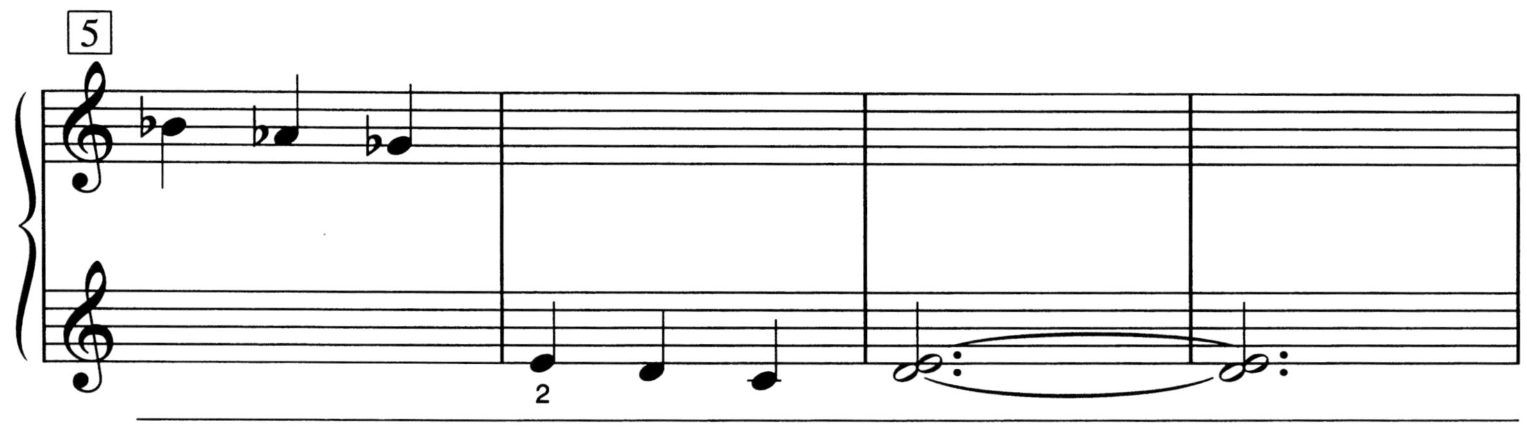

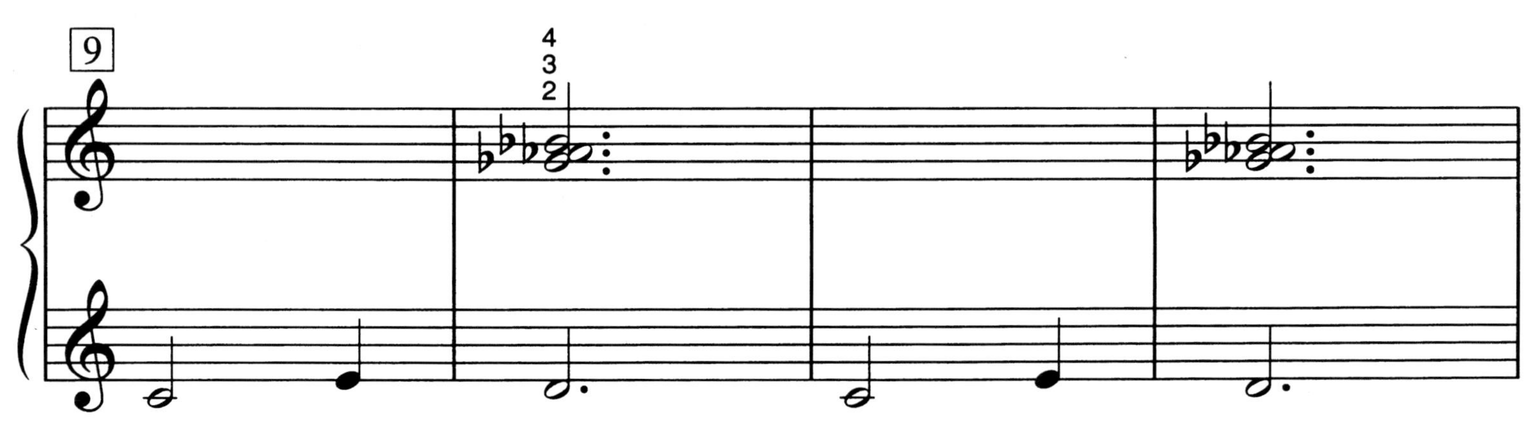

rit.
very slowly to end
r.h. over l.h.
pp
8va

Foggy Morning

ELVINA PEARCE